W9-AYK-837

math live

Numbers

David Kirkby

RIGBY
INTERACTIVE
LIBRARY

© 1996 Rigby Education
Published by Rigby Interactive Library,
an imprint of Rigby Education,
division of Reed Elsevier, Inc.
500 Coventry Lane,
Crystal Lake, IL 60014

Designed by The Point
Cover design by Pinpoint Design
Printed in the United States of America

00 99 98 97 96
10 9 8 7 6 5 4 3 2 1

Library of Congress Cataloging-in-Publication Data
Kirkby, David, 1943–
    Numbers / David Kirkby.
      p. cm. — (Math live)
    Includes index.
    Summary: Explores mathematical concepts through activities and calculations.
    ISBN 1-57572-042-6 (library)
    1. Arithmetic—Juvenile literature. [1. Arithmetic.] I. Title.
II. Series: Kirkby, David, 1943– Math live.
QA115.K57 1996
513—dc20   95–20566
                                  CIP
                                   AC

Acknowledgments
The author and publisher wish to acknowledge, with thanks, the following photographic sources:
Trevor Clifford, pp. 12, 37; all other photos: The Point.

The publisher would also like to thank the following for the kind loan of equipment:
NES Arnold Ltd; Polydron International Ltd.

> **Note to the Reader**
> In this book some words are printed in **bold** type. This indicates that the word is listed in the glossary on page 44. The glossary gives a brief explanation of words that may be new to you.

CONTENTS

1 ANCIENT NUMBERS

A long time ago, people counted using their fingers. Symbols were invented to show the numbers. The symbols are known as **numerals**.

The Maya used three symbols: the dot, the bar, and the shell.

0	1	2	3	4	5	6	7	8	9

10	11	12	13	14	15	16	17	18	19

In our number system, we move one column to the left when we reach 10. The Maya moved one rung up when they reached 20. They read their numbers from bottom to top.

$20 =$

21	22	23	24	25

$2 \times 20 = 40$	$3 \times 20 = 60$	62	$5 \times 20 = 100$

TO DO

Write the numbers 27, 80, and 101 using the Mayan system.

The Romans used several different numerals that can still be seen in some places today.

I	II	III	IV	V	VI	VII	VIII	IX	X
1	2	3	4	5	6	7	8	9	10

L	C	D	M
50	100	500	1000

The Egyptians used this system of numerals. It is probably based on drawings of fingers.

I	II	III	IIII	III II	III III	IIII III	IIII IIII	IIIII IIII	∧
1	2	3	4	5	6	7	8	9	10

∧∧∧ ∧∧	ρ	ρ ρ ρ ρ ρ	𓆼
50	100	500	1000

Both the Egyptians and the Romans added their numerals together to get larger numbers. Here is 33:

∩ ∩ ∩ III in Egyptian   XXXIII   in Roman

But the Romans found short ways of writing some numbers. They wrote:

IV for 4   XIX for 19   XC for 90

"one less than 5"   "one less than twenty"   "ten less than 100"

CHALLENGE

- Look at the fingers on one hand. What might the Roman symbol for 5 have meant? What about the one for 10?

- Write your age and birth date first in Egyptian and then in Roman numerals. How are they alike and different?

- Our numerals are called Arabic numerals. They are written in a way that makes it easy to add and subtract. Do you think this would work well with Roman numerals? Try these:

$$\begin{array}{r} IV \\ +XI \\ \hline \end{array} \qquad \begin{array}{r} XIV \\ -VI \\ \hline \end{array}$$

2 WRITING NUMBERS

Nearly 1,200 years ago, a famous Arab mathematician, Al Khowarizmi, wrote about an Indian way of writing numbers that he had discovered on his travels. His books reached continental Europe, where many Arabs lived.

Sometime later, about 800 years ago, an English monk called Abelard traveled to Europe, translated the books of Al Khowarizmi, and brought them back to England. Gradually, our way of writing numbers changed.

In fact, the numerals we use today have developed from numerals first used in India about 1,800 years ago.

Indian, 2nd century	— = ≡ ⅄ M ℓ ⁊ ⅃ 3
Indian, 9th century	۱ 2 ૨ 8 ৬ ⁊ ⌒ ૧ ০
Arabic, 10th century	۱ 2 ⅄ ⌒ ૬ 6 ⁊ 8 9 ৩
European, 12th century	۱ ৬ ૨ ⅄ ⅄ ⌐ ⁊ 8 9
European, 15th century	۱ 2 3 ৪ ૫ 6 ∧ 8 9 ০
European, 16th century	1 2 3 4 5 6 7 8 9 ◆

Since the way we write numbers comes first from the Indians and then from the Arabs, we call it the Hindu-Arabic system. In this system, we only have to use these ten numerals:
   0, 1, 2, 3, 4, 5, 6, 7, 8, and 9.

These numerals are often known as **digits**. "Digit" means "finger," so the word "digit" meaning "part of a number" probably comes from the fact that we count using fingers.

The number 57 is a two-digit number, using the two digits 5 and 7. The number 481 is a three-digit number, using the digits 4, 8, and 1.

When we write a number, such as 356, the position of each digit shows its value:

- the position of the 3 means three hundreds
- the position of the 5 means five tens
- the position of the 6 means six ones or six units.

So the positions of the digits in a three-digit number show the number of hundreds, the number of tens, and the number of units.

Hundreds	Tens	Units
3	5	6

For a four-digit number, the positions of the digits show thousands, hundreds, tens, and units.

The value of each position is ten times the value of the position to its right.

Zero is a very important digit in our number system. In the number 408, for example, the zero shows that there are no tens, and the number does not become confused with 48.

CHALLENGE

- Make four numbered cards: 2, 3, 6, 8.
- Put any two cards together to make a two-digit number.
- It is possible to make 12 different two-digit numbers. Can you find them?
- How many different three-digit numbers can you make by choosing three cards from the four?

3 ORDERING NUMBERS

A **number line** is a way of showing the order of numbers.

```
 +---+---+---+---+---+---+---+---+---+---+
 0   1   2   3   4   5   6   7   8   9   10
```

On this number line, the numbers become larger as you move from left to right.

★ CHALLENGE

Order the cards.

You need a pack of cards.

- Take out a set of ten cards numbered 1 to 10.
- Shuffle your cards, then spread them out in a straight line.

- You may swap any two cards at a time. Keep swapping until you have all the cards in the correct order.
- Count the number of swaps you needed.
- Try the activity a few more times and see what is the fewest number of swaps you need.

A number line can start and finish at any number.

$$5 \quad 6 \quad 7 \quad 8 \quad 9 \quad 10 \quad 11 \quad 12 \quad 13 \quad 14 \quad 15$$

The number 8 is less than 12, which in mathematical shorthand is written as $8 < 12$. The number 14 is greater than 10, which in mathematical shorthand is written as $14 > 10$.

So $<$ means "is less than" and $>$ means "is greater than."

The number 9 is between 7 and 11, which in mathematical shorthand is written as $7 < 9 < 11$. This reads "7 is less than 9, which is less than 11," or "9 is between 7 and 11."

TO DO

Play the Between Game.

You need three players and two number cubes.

- Take turns throwing the cubes. Add up the total number of dots each player throws.
- The winner of the round is the player whose total is between the other two. If there is a tie, throw again.
- Play ten rounds, keep score, and see who wins the most rounds.

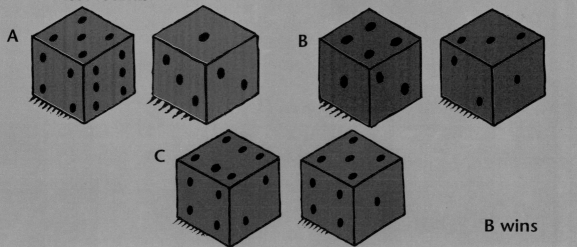

A

B

C

B wins

9

Calculator numerals do not look exactly like our written numerals. This is because they are based on a set of seven rods of equal lengths.

In a calculator display, the rods are shown by bars that light up. By lighting up some bars and not others, different numerals can be shown.

The same way of showing numerals is used in the display of a digital clock.

TO DO

- Draw the time now, using colored bars.

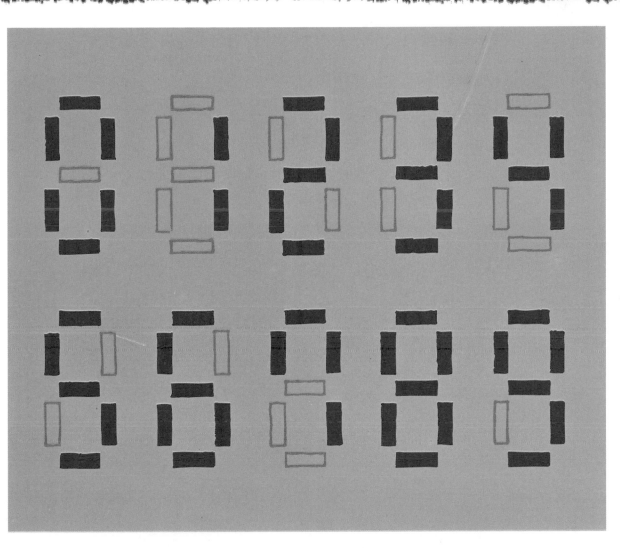

We can show the numeral 3 by lighting up five of the seven bars. *Which numeral needs the most bars lit? Which needs the fewest?* There are three numerals that need five bars lit. *Which are they?*

CHALLENGE

This calculator shows the two-digit number 44. It has a total of 8 lit bars. There are eight other two-digit numbers that need 8 lit bars. Can you find them?

ADDING

When you find the total number of objects that are in different groups, it is called **adding**. You add them together. The process of adding is called **addition**.

Annabel has 3 apples, and Paul has 5. Putting them together, there is a total of 8. When 3 and 5 are added, the total is 8. We write $3 + 5 = 8$, which reads "3 and 5 makes 8."

The + sign is called a "plus" sign. The = sign is called an "equals" sign.

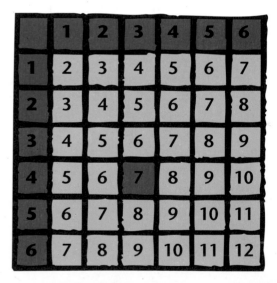

So, sometimes $3 + 5 = 8$ is read "3 plus 5 equals 8." This addition can also be written like this:

$$\begin{array}{r} 3 \\ + \ 5 \\ \hline 8 \end{array}$$

An **addition table** shows the results of adding two numbers together. The entry in the table is the total of the row heading and column heading.

For example $4 + 3 = 7$

	1	2	3	4	5	6
1	2	3	4	5	6	7
2	3	4	5	6	7	8
3	4	5	6	7	8	9
4	5	6	7	8	9	10
5	6	7	8	9	10	11
6	7	8	9	10	11	12

 TO DO

Make your own addition table with the numbers 6, 7, 8, 9, 10, and 11 as headings.

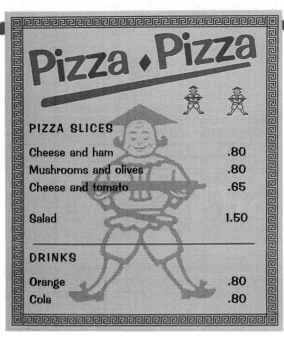

When you order a meal, you need to know how much it will cost altogether. So you need to add the prices for all the items you order.

What will it cost you for a cheese and tomato pizza slice, a salad, and an orange drink? Choose your own meal and find its cost.

TO DO

Play the Fifteens Game.

This is a game for two players. You need a set of nine cards, numbered from 1 to 9. Make a 3 by 3 square board, so that the cards will fit onto each small square.

- One player takes the even-numbered cards; the other player takes the odd-numbered cards.
- "Odd" plays first, by placing a card on one of the squares.
- Take turns placing a card.
- The winner is the first player to complete a line of three cards that total 15.

6 SUBTRACTING

If there is a collection of objects, from which you take some away, then count how many are left, you are **subtracting**. The process of subtracting is called **subtraction**.

There were 7 cakes on the plate and 2 are being taken away, which leaves 5 cakes. When 2 is subtracted from 7, the result is 5. We write $7 - 2 = 5$, which reads "7 take away 2 is 5."

The – sign is called a minus sign.
The = sign is called an "equals" sign.
So sometimes $7 - 2 = 5$ is read "7 minus 2 equals 5."
This subtraction can also be written like this:

$$\begin{array}{r} 7 \\ - \; 2 \\ \hline 5 \end{array}$$

We are also subtracting when we try to find the difference between two things.

Bejal is 48 inches tall.
Claire is 43 inches tall.
What is the difference between their heights?

In a game of darts, each player starts with a total of 301 points. On your turn, throw three darts and subtract your score from your total.

This is Lynn's first throw.
How many points has she scored with her three darts? What should she write for her score on the board? What was Dean's score on his first throw?

Dean	Lynn
301	301
270	

TO DO

Play the Subtraction Game.

This is a game for several players. You need a pack of cards without the picture cards.

- Shuffle the cards and deal three each.
- Players place their cards in this arrangement.
- The winner is the player with the largest answer to their subtraction problem.

You could play some variations of this game. The winner is the player with:

- the smallest answer
- the largest odd-numbered answer
- the smallest even-numbered answer
- the nearest answer to 40
- the nearest answer to 55.

CHALLENGE

You need four cards numbered 2, 3, 5, 8.

- Arrange the cards to make 2 two-digit numbers, then subtract the smallest from the largest. What is the answer?
- It is possible to arrange the four cards here to give twelve different answers. The smallest is 2, and the largest is 62. Try this with your selection of cards.

MULTIPLYING

Multiplying is a quick way of adding. The process of multiplying is called **multiplication**.

There are 6 pieces of chocolate in each row. There are 3 rows. So altogether there are 3 sets of 6 pieces, which is 18 pieces. We say that "6 multiplied by 3 is 18," or "6 times 3 = 18," and we write 6 x 3 = 18. This multiplication can also be written like this:

$$\begin{array}{r} 6 \\ \times\ 3 \\ \hline 18 \end{array}$$

The set of cubes on the left shows that 3 multiplied by 4 is 12, or 3 x 4 = 12. *What multiplications do the other two sets of cubes show?*

The first set of stamps shows that 5 multiplied by 3 is 15. The other shows that 3 multiplied by 5 is 15. So 3 x 5 = 15, and 5 x 3 = 15.

The result of a multiplication is called the **product**. So we say that "the product of 3 and 5 is 15."

What multiplications do these bottles show?

CHALLENGE

Make a multiplication square.

- Copy the large square on the right.
- Choose any small square.
- Imagine that it is a corner of a rectangle, and that the other corner is on the top left of the large square.

- Count the number of squares inside the rectangle. Write it in the small square.
- Continue until you have filled all the small squares.

8 DIVIDING

When things are shared out, it is called **dividing**.
The process of dividing is called **division**.

This picture shows how 15 cookies have been divided
equally among 3 plates. Each person's share is 5 cookies.
So 15 has been divided by 3, to give 5 to each.
We write 15 ÷ 3 = 5, which reads "15 divided by 3 is 5."
We say that "15 is exactly divisible by 3."

Division is very closely linked to multiplication.

How many marbles can you see?
The marbles are in 5 groups, with 4 in each group.

The total number of marbles is found by multiplying
5 by 4 or 5 x 4 = 20
20 marbles divided by 5 groups tells you how many in
each group. 20 ÷ 5 = 4
20 marbles divided by 4 in each group tells you the
number of groups. 20 ÷ 4 = 5
So for every multiplication fact, there are two linked
division facts.

1	2	3	4	5	6	7	8	9	10
2	4	6	8	10	12	14	16	18	20
3	6	9	12	15	18	21	24	27	30
4	8	12	16	20	24	28	32	36	40
5	10	15	20	25	30	35	40	45	50
6	12	18	24	30	36	42	48	54	60
7	14	21	28	35	42	49	56	63	70
8	16	24	32	40	48	56	64	72	80
9	18	27	36	45	54	63	72	81	90
10	20	30	40	50	60	70	80	90	100

Every multiplication fact in the multiplication square leads to two linked division facts. The highlighted square, for example, shows the multiplication fact, 5 x 7 = 35. From this we know that 35 ÷ 5 = 7 and 35 ÷ 7 = 5.

TO DO

- Use the multiplication square to find ten numbers that are exactly divisible by 6.
- Write down the 20 division facts.

Sometimes things divide exactly, and sometimes they do not. If you are sharing some toffees, for example, and they do not divide exactly, then you may have one or two toffees left over. This is called a **remainder**.

In this picture, 14 toffees have been divided by 4 to give 3 each, and there is a remainder of 2. We write 14 ÷ 4 = 3, remainder 2.

CHALLENGE

Which numbers in the multiplication square will leave a remainder of 1 when divided by 5?

Each of these sets of squares shows a different multiplication by 3. They are:

1 times 3 is 3	or	1 x 3 = 3
2 times 3 is 6	or	2 x 3 = 6
3 times 3 is 9	or	3 x 3 = 9
4 times 3 is 12	or	4 x 3 = 12
5 times 3 is 15	or	5 x 3 = 15
6 times 3 is 18	or	6 x 3 = 18

This is called a **multiplication table** for multiplying by 3. It is sometimes called a times table for multiplying by 3, or a 3 times table.

The factbox gives some more multiplication tables.

FACTBOX			
1 x 8 = 8	1 x 3 = 3	1 x 5 = 5	1 x 7 = 7
2 x 8 = 16	2 x 3 = 6	2 x 5 = 10	2 x 7 = 14
3 x 8 = 24	3 x 3 = 9	3 x 5 = 15	3 x 7 = 21
4 x 8 = 32	4 x 3 = 12	4 x 5 = 20	4 x 7 = 28
5 x 8 = 40	5 x 3 = 15	5 x 5 = 25	5 x 7 = 35
6 x 8 = 48	6 x 3 = 18	6 x 5 = 30	6 x 7 = 42
7 x 8 = 56	7 x 3 = 21	7 x 5 = 35	7 x 7 = 49
8 x 8 = 64	8 x 3 = 24	8 x 5 = 40	8 x 7 = 56
9 x 8 = 72	9 x 3 = 27	9 x 5 = 45	9 x 7 = 63
10 x 8 = 80	10 x 3 = 30	10 x 5 = 50	10 x 7 = 70

CHALLENGE

Here are the next five lines of the 3 times table. What are the next five lines of the other tables?

11 x 3 = 33
12 x 3 = 36
13 x 3 = 39
14 x 3 = 42
15 x 3 = 45

1	2	3	4	5	6	7	8	9	10
2	4	6	8	10	12	14	16	18	20
3	6	9	12	15	18	21	24	27	30
4	8	12	16	20	24	28	32	36	40
5	10	15	20	25	30	35	40	45	50
6	12	18	24	30	36	42	48	54	60
7	14	21	28	35	42	49	56	63	70
8	16	24	32	40	48	56	64	72	80
9	18	27	36	45	54	63	72	81	90
10	20	30	40	50	60	70	80	90	100

The rows and columns of a multiplication square show all the multiplication tables for multiplying by 1 up to multiplying by 10. If you look down the fourth column, you see the results of multiplying by 4.

Look carefully at the multiplication square, and you will see that some numbers appear several times. For example, the number 12 appears four times, and the number 16 appears three times.

CHALLENGE

- Apart from number 12, there are seven more numbers that appear four times. Can you spot them?
- Apart from number 16, there are three more numbers that appear three times. Can you spot these?
- There are nineteen numbers up to 50 that do not appear at all. They are, in order:

11	13				23		29			34				41				47

Can you fill in the gaps?

10 MULTIPLES

The **multiples** of 3 are the results of multiplying different numbers by 3. So the multiples of 3 are 3, 6, 9, 12, 15, and so on. To show the multiples of 3, draw a 3-row grid and write the numbers in order, starting at 1, like this:

1	4	7	10	13	16	19	22	25	28
2	5	8	11	14	17	20	23	26	29
3	6	9	12	15	18	21	24	27	30

FACTBOX
1 x 3 = **3**
2 x 3 = **6**
3 x 3 = **9**
4 x 3 = **12**
5 x 3 = **15**
6 x 3 = **18**
7 x 3 = **21**
8 x 3 = **24**
9 x 3 = **27**
10 x 3 = **30**

The multiples of 3 will appear in the bottom row.

TO DO

Use the same method to show the multiples of 7. You will need to draw a 7-row grid on graph paper.

The multiples of 3 make an interesting pattern on a hundred square. *How would you describe the pattern?*

1	2	3	4	5	6	7	8	9	10
11	12	13	14	15	16	17	18	19	20
21	22	23	24	25	26	27	28	29	30
31	32	33	34	35	36	37	38	39	40
41	42	43	44	45	46	47	48	49	50
51	52	53	54	55	56	57	58	59	60
61	62	63	64	65	66	67	68	69	70
71	72	73	74	75	76	77	78	79	80
81	82	83	84	85	86	87	88	89	90
91	92	93	94	95	96	97	98	99	100

The multiples of other numbers are found by looking along the rows or down the columns of a multiplication square. So the multiples of 7, for instance, are 7, 14, 21, 28, 35, and so on.

Notice that 15 is a multiple of 5, and also that 15 is a multiple of 3. So 15 is a common multiple of 3 and 5.

18 is a multiple of 6, and 18 is also a multiple of 9. So 18 is a common multiple of 6 and 9.

1	2	3	4	5	6	7	8	9	10
2	4	6	8	10	12	14	16	18	20
3	6	9	12	15	18	21	24	27	30
4	8	12	16	20	24	28	32	36	40
5	10	15	20	25	30	35	40	45	50
6	12	18	24	30	36	42	48	54	60
7	14	21	28	35	42	49	56	63	70
8	16	24	32	40	48	56	64	72	80
9	18	27	36	45	54	63	72	81	90
10	20	30	40	50	60	70	80	90	100

CHALLENGE

Find two numbers in the multiplication square that are common multiples of 4 and 5.

TO DO

Play "Up the Multiples of 3, Down the Multiples of 5."
This is a game for two players.

START	1	2	3	4	5	6	7	8	9	10	11	12	13
28	27	26	25	24	23	22	21	20	19	18	17	16	15	14
29	30	31	32	33	34	35	36	37	38	39	40	41	42	43
58	57	56	55	54	53	52	51	50	49	48	47	46	45	44
59	60	61	62	63	64	65	66	67	68	69	70	FINISH		

- Place your counters at "Start."
- Take turns throwing a number cube, and move that number of spaces around the board.
- If you land on a multiple of 3, jump forward to the next multiple of 3.
- If you land on a multiple of 5, jump backward to the previous multiple of 5.
- The winner is the first to reach "Finish."

Play again, choosing different multiples for "up" and "down."

11 FACTORS

The number 18 can be divided exactly by six numbers, 1, 2, 3, 6, 9, and 18. The numbers 1, 2, 3, 6, 9, and 18 are called the **factors** of 18. The number 18 has six factors.

The factors of a number are all the numbers that will divide into it exactly. Because 3 is a factor of 18, it follows that 18 is a multiple of 3.

12 flower pots have been arranged in different ways. The picture shows them arranged in:

- 2 rows of 6 pots, which shows that 2 and 6 are a pair of factors of 12
- 3 rows of 4 pots, which shows that 3 and 4 are a pair of factors of 12
- 1 row of 12 pots, which shows that 1 and 12 are a pair of factors of 12

So 12 has three pairs of factors.

TO DO

You need some counters to stand for your flower pots.

- Start with 20 counters.
- Find different ways of arranging them in equal rows.
- Write down the pair of factors shown by each arrangement.
- Finally, list all the factors of 20.

Try again, with a different number of counters.

FACTBOX

Number	Factors	Number	Factors
1	1	16	1, 2, 4, 8, 16
2	1, 2	17	1, 17
3	1, 3	18	1, 2, 3, 6, 9, 18
4	1, 2, 4	19	1, 19
5	1, 5	20	1, 2, 4, 5, 10, 20
6	1, 2, 3, 6	21	1, 3, 7, 21
7	1, 7	22	1, 2, 11, 22
8	1, 2, 4, 8	23	1, 23
9	1, 3, 9	24	1, 2, 3, 4, 6, 8, 12, 24
10	1, 2, 5, 10	25	1, 5, 25
11	1, 11	26	1, 2, 13, 26
12	1, 2, 3, 4, 6, 12	27	1, 3, 9, 27
13	1, 13	28	1, 2, 4, 7, 14, 28
14	1, 2, 7, 14	29	1, 29
15	1, 3, 5, 15	30	1, 2, 3, 5, 6, 10, 15, 30

Notice that 1 is a factor of every number. Notice, too, that every number is a factor of itself. For example, 10 is a factor of 10.

CHALLENGE

The number 3 is a factor of 6 and a factor of 21. So 3 is a common factor of 6 and 21. Can you find some common factors of 20 and 24, 8 and 18, 15 and 10, 16 and 30?

TO DO

Play the Factor Game.

- Shuffle a set of cards numbered 1 to 9.
- Each player makes a scoresheet like the one shown.
- Deal out four of the cards, such as:

- Using these four digits only, and not using any one of them more than four times altogether, see how many two-digit numbers you can complete correctly on the scoresheet.

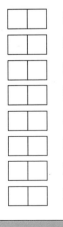

Factor Game Scoresheet

	has a factor of 2
	has a factor of 3
	has a factor of 4
	has a factor of 5
	has a factor of 6
	has a factor of 7
	has a factor of 8
	has a factor of 9

25

12 PRIME NUMBERS

A **prime number** is a number that has exactly two factors, itself and 1. For example, the only factors of 7 are 1 and 7. The only factors of 11 are 1 and 11. So 7 and 11 are prime numbers.

7	17	13
11	37	**5**

Prime numbers can be found by using the **Sieve of Eratosthenes**. Eratosthenes, a Greek mathematician who lived in about 200 B.C.E., devised the following method for finding prime numbers.

TO DO

You need counters of five different colors.

- Start with a hundred square.
- Place one colored counter on the number 1.
- Place counters of the next color on the multiples of 2, except 2 itself.
- Place counters of the next color on the multiples of 3, except 3 itself.
- Place counters of the next color on the multiples of 5, except 5 itself.
- Finally, place counters of the last color on the multiples of 7, except 7 itself.

1	2	3	4	5	6	7	8	9	10
11	12	13	14	15	16	17	18	19	20
21	22	23	24	25	26	27	28	29	30
31	32	33	34	35	36	37	38	39	40
41	42	43	44	45	46	47	48	49	50
51	52	53	54	55	56	57	58	59	60
61	62	63	64	65	66	67	68	69	70
71	72	73	74	75	76	77	78	79	80
81	82	83	84	85	86	87	88	89	90
91	92	93	94	95	96	97	98	99	100

The numbers that have counters on them have been sifted out. The numbers that are left without a counter are the prime numbers up to 100. How many are there?

Numbers that are not prime numbers can be arranged to form a square or rectangle.

6

9

20

These numbers have more than two factors. Prime numbers cannot be arranged to form a square or rectangle.

If the numbers from 1 to 100 are written, in order, in six columns, and then the prime numbers are highlighted, an interesting pattern can be seen.

This shows that, apart from the first two prime numbers, 2 and 3, they all lie in either the first or fifth column.

In other words, they are all either one more or one less than a multiple of 6.

Notice that 2 is the only even prime number. Notice, too, that all prime numbers have 1, 3, 7, or 9 as their last digit.

1	2	3	4	5	6
7	8	9	10	11	12
13	14	15	16	17	18
19	20	21	22	23	24
25	26	27	28	29	30
31	32	33	34	35	36
37	38	39	40	41	42
43	44	45	46	47	48
49	50	51	52	53	54
55	56	57	58	59	60
61	62	63	64	65	66
67	68	69	70	71	72
73	74	75	76	77	78
79	80	81	82	83	84
85	86	87	88	89	90
91	92	93	94	95	96
97	98	99	100		

CHALLENGE

- Can you write the first ten prime numbers without looking at this book?
- Now can you write the next five?

13 SQUARE NUMBERS

If a number of pegs can be placed on a pegboard to make a square, then the number of pegs used is called a **square number**.

These three pegboards show 9 pegs, 25 pegs, and 16 pegs, in turn, arranged in squares. They show that 9, 25, and 16 are square numbers.

The square numbers are the results of the multiplication facts: 1 x 1, 2 x 2, 3 x 3, 4 x 4, and so on.
They are 1, 4, 9, 16, 25, 36, 49, 64, 81, 100, and so on.

We write:
- $2^2 = 4$, and say "two squared is four"
- $3^2 = 9$, and say "three squared is nine"
- $4^2 = 16$, and say "four squared is sixteen"
- $5^2 = 25$, and say "five squared is twenty-five"

1	2	3	4	5	6	7	8	9	10
2	4	6	8	10	12	14	16	18	20
3	6	9	12	15	18	21	24	27	30
4	8	12	16	20	24	28	32	36	40
5	10	15	20	25	30	35	40	45	50
6	12	18	24	30	36	42	48	54	60
7	14	21	28	35	42	49	56	63	70
8	16	24	32	40	48	56	64	72	80
9	18	27	36	45	54	63	72	81	90
10	20	30	40	50	60	70	80	90	100

Note their position on the multiplication square. They lie along a diagonal line.

This picture shows a set of differently sized squares, each with a corner in the top left. Look at the picture so that you can see the different square numbers.

TO DO

• Notice that you can build up one square number from another by adding on some pegs.

Write the square numbers

1   4   9   16   25   36   49 . . .

Write the differences

(+3) (+5) (+7) (+9) (+11) (+13) . . .

• Notice also that $4 = 1 + 3$
                     $9 = 1 + 3 + 5$
               $16 = 1 + 3 + 5 + 7$

Write the next three square numbers like this.
Can you see another pattern?

TO DO

• Make your own number spiral like this on graph paper, then color all the square numbers.
• What pattern do the square numbers make?

		26	27	28	29	30	31		
		25	10	11	12	13	32		
		24	9	2	3	14	33		
		23	8	1	4	15	34		
		22	7	6	5	16	35		
		21	20	19	18	17	36		
							37		

14 FRACTIONS

A **fraction** is a part of a whole. For example, if you slice a pizza into two equal pieces, then each piece is called one half. If, instead, you slice it into three equal pieces, each is called one third. If four people are going to share the pizza, then you need four equal pieces, and each piece is called one quarter. One half, one third, and one quarter are all examples of fractions.

The fraction one half is written as $\frac{1}{2}$.
One third is written $\frac{1}{3}$ and one quarter is written $\frac{1}{4}$.

Other examples of fractions are shown in the factbox.

FACTBOX		
Number of equal parts of a whole	**Fraction of each part**	
2	one half	$\frac{1}{2}$
3	one third	$\frac{1}{3}$
4	one quarter	$\frac{1}{4}$
5	one fifth	$\frac{1}{5}$
6	one sixth	$\frac{1}{6}$
7	one seventh	$\frac{1}{7}$
8	one eighth	$\frac{1}{8}$
9	one ninth	$\frac{1}{9}$
10	one tenth	$\frac{1}{10}$

TO DO

Find different halves.

You need some graph paper.

- Draw some 4 by 4 squares.
- Here are three ways of halving the square.
- How many other ways can you find?

The cake has been divided into three thirds. There is one third on the right, and two thirds on the left. We write these fractions as $\frac{1}{3}$ and $\frac{2}{3}$.

Fractions of each shape have been colored.
The fractions are three quarters of the square, two fifths of the pentagon, five sixths of the hexagon and seven eighths of the rectangle.
Can you say what fraction of each shape is not colored?

 CHALLENGE

Each of these squares has been divided into parts.
The lines drawn to the sides of each square meet the sides halfway. Can you say what fraction each part is of each square? One is done for you.

31

15 EQUIVALENT FRACTIONS

Different fractions can sometimes mean the
same part of a whole.

For example, the drawing shows that one half is the same
as two quarters, which is the same as four eighths of the
rectangle.

So $\frac{1}{2}$, $\frac{2}{4}$ and $\frac{4}{8}$ are called **equivalent fractions**.

One way of showing equivalent fractions is to build a
fraction wall. Each layer of the wall is one whole, and this is
marked on the bottom layer. The other layers are divided
into equal parts, and their fractions are marked on the wall.

From the wall you can see that $\frac{1}{2}$ is equivalent to $\frac{2}{4}$, which is
equivalent to $\frac{4}{8}$.

$\frac{1}{4}$ and $\frac{2}{8}$ are also equivalent fractions.

So are $\frac{3}{4}$ and $\frac{6}{8}$.

1	2	3	4	5	6	7	8	9	10
2	4	6	8	10	12	14	16	18	20
3	6	9	12	15	18	21	24	27	30
4	8	12	16	20	24	28	32	36	40
5	10	15	20	25	30	35	40	45	50
6	12	18	24	30	36	42	48	54	60
7	14	21	28	35	42	49	56	63	70
8	16	24	32	40	48	56	64	72	80
9	18	27	36	45	54	63	72	81	90
10	20	30	40	50	60	70	80	90	100

A good way of finding sets of equivalent fractions is to use a multiplication square.

To find some fractions equivalent to $\frac{2}{5}$, look along the 2 row, and also along the 5 row.

Pairing the numbers, one from each row, gives this set of equivalent fractions: $\frac{2}{5} = \frac{4}{10} = \frac{6}{15} = \frac{8}{20} = \frac{10}{25}$ and so on.

CHALLENGE

Use the multiplication square to find some fractions equivalent to $\frac{3}{4}$ and also to $\frac{5}{6}$.

TO DO

Make some equivalent fractions.

- Take a piece of paper.
- Fold it in half, then in half again, and finally once more, so that the folds are as shown above.
- Open out the paper and mark each section with its fraction of the whole piece of paper.
- Can you use this paper to show some equivalent fractions?

Experiment by folding other pieces of paper in different ways, looking for equivalent fractions.

16 DECIMALS

Our way of writing numbers is based on the position of the digits 0, 1, 2, 3, 4, 5, 6, 7, 8, and 9. So, for example, 273 means 2 hundreds, 7 tens, and 3 ones, and is read "two hundred seventy-three."

Thousands	Hundreds	Tens	Ones
	2	7	3

The value of each position is ten times the value of the position to the right. So if we continue the order:

hundreds, tens, ones ...

then the value of the next position is tenths.

To separate the whole numbers from the fraction, a point is placed between them. This is known as a **decimal point**, and a number that has a decimal point is called a **decimal number**. For example, 358.6 means 3 hundreds, 5 tens, 8 ones, and 6 tenths, and is read "three hundred fifty-eight point six."

Thousands	Hundreds	Tens	Ones	Tenths
	3	5	8 •	6

Sometimes a number has no whole numbers, just tenths. 0.3 means 0 ones and 3 tenths, and is read "zero point three."

CHALLENGE

You need four numbered cards.

1 4 6 9

- On a large piece of paper, draw boxes for a decimal number like this:
- Choose two cards to make a decimal number with ones and tenths.
- It is possible to make 12 different decimal numbers. Can you find them?
- Put them in order, from smallest to largest.

Just as with whole numbers, we can show decimal numbers on number lines.

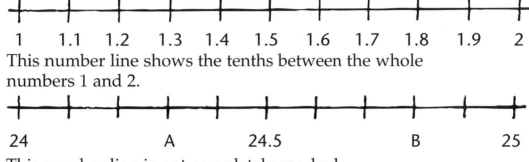

1   1.1   1.2   1.3   1.4   1.5   1.6   1.7   1.8   1.9   2

This number line shows the tenths between the whole numbers 1 and 2.

24   A   24.5   B   25

This number line is not completely marked.
What numbers on the line do A and B stand for?

The markings on this ruler show another number line, marked in centimeters and millimeters. There are 10 millimeters in each centimeter, so each millimeter is one tenth of a centimeter.

The pencil measures 8.7 centimeters.

TO DO

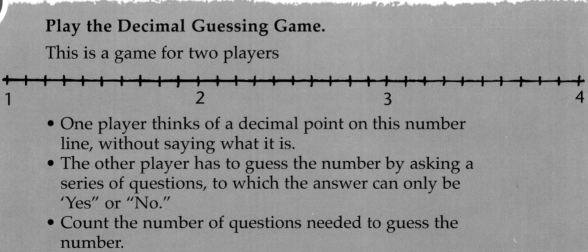

Play the Decimal Guessing Game.

This is a game for two players

1   2   3   4

• One player thinks of a decimal point on this number line, without saying what it is.
• The other player has to guess the number by asking a series of questions, to which the answer can only be 'Yes" or "No."
• Count the number of questions needed to guess the number.
• Then swap roles and see who needs the fewer questions.

35

17 HUNDREDTHS

The square on the left has been divided into 10 equal parts. Each strip is one tenth of the square. The square on the right has been divided into 100 equal parts. Each small square is one hundredth of the large square. The colored parts of each square show that ten hundredths is the same as one tenth.

We know that when numbers are written, the value of each position is ten times the value of the position to the right.

So if we continue the order:
hundreds, tens, ones, tenths . . .
then the value of the next position is hundredths.

For example, the decimal number 27.48 means 2 tens, 7 ones, 4 tenths, and 8 hundredths, and is read "twenty-seven point four eight."

Thousands	Hundreds	Tens	Ones	Tenths	Hundredths
		2	7	4	8

Sprint races are measured in hundredths of a second. These are some runners' times:

Smith   10.23 seconds   Brown   10.04 seconds
Levin   9.93 seconds   Yung   9.50 seconds
Kelly   9.86 seconds

Who won? What were the positions of the other athletes?

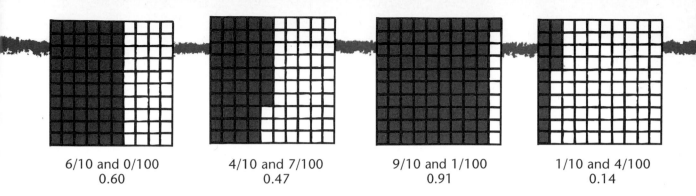

| 6/10 and 0/100 | 4/10 and 7/100 | 9/10 and 1/100 | 1/10 and 4/100 |
| 0.60 | 0.47 | 0.91 | 0.14 |

The first position after the decimal point shows tenths. The second position after the decimal point shows hundredths. These are sometimes called the first decimal place and the second decimal place.
What do you think will be the value of the third decimal place?

TO DO

Find some graph paper, and cut out four 10 by 10 squares.

• Color fractions of each square to show the decimal numbers 0.35, 0.86, 0.7, and 0.4.

Height can be measured in meters and centimeters. There are 100 centimeters in each meter, so each centimeter is one hundredth of a meter.

Siobhan's height is 112 centimeters.
So she is 1 meter and 12 centimeters tall
Her height is 1.12 meters.

TO DO

• Find a metric measure, and measure the heights of family and friends.
• Write their heights in meters using decimal numbers.

18 ROUNDING

Sometimes, instead of writing a number exactly, we round it. There are different ways of rounding a number.

We can round up to the next 10, so that:

    14 becomes 20   28 becomes 30   62 becomes 70
    79 becomes 80   *What happens to 36 and 81?*

We can round down to the previous 10, so that:

    14 becomes 10   28 becomes 20   62 becomes 60
    79 becomes 70   *What happens to 33 and 58?*

We can round to the nearest 10, so that:

14 becomes 10   28 becomes 30   62 becomes 60
79 becomes 80   *What happens to 57 and 73?*

We sometimes round a measurement to the nearest unit.
What is the length of the cucumber to the nearest inch?
What is the weight of the potatoes to the nearest pound?

TO DO

- Measure your height, rounded to the nearest inch.
- Measure your weight, rounded to the nearest pound.

Sometimes, especially when numbers are large, we do not need to know the exact size of a number, but need a rough idea of its size. So we round the number. This is called approximating.

For example, if the number of people who watched a baseball game was 17, 472, we can approximate it to the nearest thousand: 17, 000. We can approximate it to the nearest hundred: 17, 500. Or we can approximate it to the nearest ten: 17, 470.

CHALLENGE

- Can you round the attendance figures at each game to the nearest thousand?
- Now try it to the nearest hundred.

Sox v Yankees	33,648
Astros v Dodgers	36,329
Cubs v Giants	34,793
Twins v Orioles	26,522

TO DO

You need a stopwatch on a digital watch.
- Set the stopwatch to zero.
    00:00 00
- Start it, then after a short while, stop it.
    00:16 79
- Write down the time on the watch.
- Write down the number of seconds that have passed.
- Round it to the nearest second.

Stopwatch Time	Number of Seconds	Nearest Second
00:16:79	16.79	17

- Try some more times.

19 PERCENTAGES

A **percentage** is a fraction of 100. 100 percent is the whole amount.

The fraction thirteen hundredths ($\frac{13}{100}$) is the percentage 13. We say it is "thirteen percent," and we write 13%. The fraction forty-seven hundredths ($\frac{47}{100}$) is the percentage 47. We say it is "forty-seven percent" and we write 47%.

In each of these squares, a different percentage has been colored:

60%

32%

Well known fractions of these squares have been colored:

one quarter, $\frac{1}{4}$ is 25%

one half, $\frac{1}{2}$ is 50%

three quarters, $\frac{3}{4}$ is 75%

There are 10 candies in this picture. So each candy is 10% of the total (100%). 20% are green.

What percentages are yellow, red, and pink?

> Holly pulled herself into a ball on the floor of the garage and waited for the shuddering to stop.
>
> 'Wake up!' Jamie ran back and crouched over her. 'Holly, wake up!'
>
> 'It's OK, look, she's breathing!' There was

Letters are either vowels – a, e, i, o, u – or consonants. When we write, do we use more vowels than consonants? Look at this passage of writing. The two lines are drawn to mark off the first 100 letters. There are 38 vowels. Count them to check. There are 62 consonants. So, of these 100 letters, 38% are vowels, and 62% are consonants.

CHALLENGE

- Find your own page of writing.
- Mark off the first 100 letters.
- Find the percentage of vowels and the percentage of consonants.
- How do they compare with the percentages given above?

TO DO

Which colors of car do you think are most popular?
- Record the color of the first 100 cars you see.
- Start by making a chart to keep a record.

Color	Tally	Percentage
White	⊞⊞ II	
Black	⊞⊞	
Blue	⊞⊞ IIII	
Red	⊞⊞ I	
...		

- Stop when you have recorded the colors of 100 cars.
- Then write down the percentage of each color.
- What are your conclusions?

A **number line** is used to show how numbers are ordered.

A number line is infinitely long, which means that it can be extended in both directions forever. As we move along the line from left to right, the numbers get larger. As we move along the line from right to left, the numbers get smaller, and eventually reach 0.

As we count from right to left, the numbers are 6, 5, 4, 3, 2, 1, and then 0. Then, counting past 0, the next number is −1, then −2, then −3, and so on. We say these numbers as "negative one," "negative two," "negative three," or as "minus one," "minus two," and "minus three."

The numbers below 0 are called **negative numbers**, while those above zero are called **positive numbers**.

A thermometer is an instrument for measuring temperature. The scale on a thermometer is like a number line. Temperature is measured in degrees Fahrenheit (°F) or Celcius (°C).

On a warm day, the temperature is about 75 °F, but in the winter, when the weather is much colder, the temperature comes down, sometimes as far as 0 °F, and sometimes even further.

A temperature of 0 °F is very cold, but temperatures can go even lower. A temperature of − 3 °F, for example, is said to be "3 degrees below zero."

Positive and negative numbers can be added together.
For example, the result of adding −2 and 3 is 1,
while the result of adding 1 and −4 is −3. A simple way of
showing this is to jump along a number line.

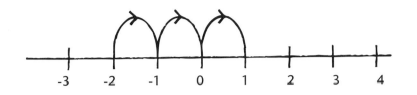

When you add a positive number, jump right.
When you add a negative number, jump left.

To add −2 and 3, start at the first number, −2, then jump 3
spaces right.
To add 1 and −4, start at the first number, 1, then jump 4
spaces left.

CHALLENGE

• Make nine number cards like this:

• Make addition sums using three
cards, like this:

• How many different additions
can you make?

GLOSSARY

adding   Finding the total number of objects in different groups.

addition   The process of **adding**.

addition table   A number table that allows you to see the result of **adding** two numbers together.

decimal number   A number that is partly a whole number and partly a **fraction**.

decimal point   A point used to separate the whole numbers from the **fraction** in a **decimal number**.

digit   A **numeral** used as part of a number.

dividing   Sharing a group of objects equally.

division   The process of **dividing**.

equivalent fractions   Different **fractions** that are the same part of a whole.

factor   The factors of a number are those numbers that will divide into it exactly.

fraction   A part of a whole.

multiples   The multiples of a number are those that can be evenly divided by that number. For example, the multiples of 9 are 9, 18, 27, and so on.

multiplication   The process of **multiplying**.

multiplication table   A number table that allows you to see the result of **multiplying** two numbers together.

multiplying   **Adding** several groups of objects each of which contains the same number.

negative numbers   Numbers less than zero.

number line   A straight line with equal divisions to show numbers in order.

numerals   Symbols used to show a number.

percentage   A number of hundredths of a whole.

positive numbers   Numbers more than zero.

prime number	A number that has exactly two factors, itself and 1.
product	The result of a **multiplication**.
remainder	The objects left when a **division** will not give exactly equal shares.
Sieve of Eratosthenes	A method for finding **prime numbers**.
square number	The result of **multiplying** a number by itself.
subtracting	Taking a number of objects away from a group and counting the number left.
subtraction	The process of **subtracting**.

INDEX

ANSWERS

p. 4
To Do

27   80   101

p. 5
Challenge: XV, VIII

p. 7

2	3	2	6	2	8	3	6	3	8	6	8
3	2	6	2	8	2	6	3	8	3	8	6

p.11
Most: 8; fewest: 1; five bars: 2, 3, 5.

There are 24 possible combinations of 3 cards.

Challenge: 10, 16, 19, 47, 61, 74, 77, 91

p.13
It will cost you $2.95.

p.14
5 inches.

p.15
Lynn has scored 25 points. Her score should now read 276. Dean's score on his first throw was 31.

p.16
The other multiplications show 5 x 60 and 7 x 2.

p.17
The crate of bottles shows the multiplication 5 x 4.

p.18
There are 20 marbles.

p.19
To Do: The numbers exactly divisible by 6 are: 6, 12, 18, 24, 30, 36, 42, 48, 54, 60.

Challenge: The numbers that will leave a remainder of 1 are: 6, 16, 21, 36, 56, 81.

p.20
The next five lines of the other times tables are:
11 x 8 = 88   11 x 5 = 55   11 x 7 = 77
12 x 8 = 96   12 x 5 = 60   12 x 7 = 84
13 x 8 = 104   13 x 5 = 65   13 x 7 = 91
14 x 8 = 112   14 x 5 = 70   14 x 7 = 98
15 x 8 = 120   15 x 5 = 75   15 x 7 = 105

p.21
The seven other numbers that appear four times are 6, 8, 18, 20, 24, 30, 40. The three other numbers that appear three times are: 4, 9, 36. The numbers that do not appear are: 11, 13, 17, 19, 22, 23, 26, 29, 31, 33, 34, 37, 38, 39, 41, 43, 44, 46, 47.

p.23
Challenge: The two numbers that are common multiples of 4 and 5 are: 20, 40.

p.24 The factors of 20 are: 1, 2, 4, 5, 10.

p.25 **Challenge**
Common factors of 20 and 24: 1, 2, 4
Common factors of 8 and 18: 1, 2
Common factors of 15 and 10: 1, 5
Common factors of 16 and 30: 1, 2

p.26 **To Do**
There are 25 prime numbers.

Challenge
The first 10 prime numbers are: 1, 2, 3, 5, 7, 11, 13, 17, 19, 23. The next 5 are: 29, 31, 37, 41, 43.

p.31 $\frac{1}{4}, \frac{3}{5}, \frac{1}{6}, \frac{1}{8}$

Challenge
The fractions are: $\frac{1}{2}, \frac{1}{2}$. $\frac{1}{2}, \frac{1}{4}, \frac{1}{4}$. $\frac{1}{4}, \frac{1}{4}, \frac{1}{4}, \frac{1}{4}$. $\frac{1}{2}, \frac{1}{4}, \frac{1}{4}$.

$\frac{1}{4}, \frac{1}{4}, \frac{1}{2}$. $\frac{1}{4}, \frac{1}{4}, \frac{1}{4}, \frac{1}{8}, \frac{1}{8}$. $\frac{1}{8}, \frac{3}{8}, \frac{1}{4}, \frac{1}{4}$. $\frac{1}{8}, \frac{7}{8}$.

p.33 **Challenge**
The equivalent fractions of $\frac{3}{4}$ are: $\frac{6}{8}, \frac{9}{12}, \frac{12}{16}, \frac{15}{20}, \frac{18}{24}, \frac{21}{28}, \frac{24}{32}, \frac{27}{36}, \frac{30}{40}$

The equivalent fractions of $\frac{5}{6}$ are: $\frac{10}{12}, \frac{15}{18}, \frac{20}{24}, \frac{25}{30}, \frac{30}{36}, \frac{35}{42}, \frac{40}{48}, \frac{45}{54}, \frac{50}{60}$

p.34 **Challenge**
The 12 possible decimal numbers are: 1·4, 1·6, 1·9, 4·1, 4·6, 4·9, 6·1, 6·4, 6·9, 9·1, 9·4, 9·6.

p.35 A stands for 24·3   B stands for 24·8

p.36 1st: Yung; 2nd: Kelly; 3rd: Levin; 4th: Brown; 5th: Smith

p.37 The value of the third decimal place is thousandths.

p.38
36 becomes 40	33 becomes 30	57 becomes 60
81 becomes 90	58 becomes 50	73 becomes 70

Cucumber is about 5 in; potatoes weigh about 1lb.

p.39 **Challenge**
Sox v Yankees	34,000; 33,600
Astros v Dodgers	36,000; 36,300
Cubs v Giants	35,000; 34,800
Twins v Orioles	27,000; 26,500

p.40 Yellow: 40%   Red: 30%   Pink: 10%

p.43 **Challenge**
You can make 72 possible additions.